BEHOLD THE OCTOPUS!

With love to Aunt Jean, Cindy, and Courtney
—S. S.

Thank you to the researchers who strive to
understand our planet and its inhabitants, and to
my wife Noni and daughter Nina who allow me
the time to work on such wonderful books
—T. G.

Published by
PEACHTREE PUBLISHING COMPANY INC.
1700 Chattahoochee Avenue
Atlanta, Georgia 30318-2112
PeachtreeBooks.com

Text © 2023 by Suzanne Slade
Illustrations © 2023 by Thomas Gonzalez

Edited by Kathy Landwehr
Design and composition by Adela Pons

Illustrations created in pastel, colored pencils, and airbrush.

Printed and bound in December 2022 at Toppan Leefung, DongGuan, China.
10 9 8 7 6 5 4 3 2 1
First Edition
ISBN: 978-1-68263-312-0

Cataloging-in-Publication Data is available from the Library of Congress.

Photo credits
page 28: Mimic octopus (*Thaumoctopus mimicus*) in the Lembeh Strait,
Sulawesi, Indonesia (Shutterstock 111383873); A Coconut Octopus
hides inside a broken glass bottle on a black sandy seabed (Shutterstock
257419795)
page 29: Star-sucker Pygmy Octopus (aka Wolfs Pygmy Octopus -
Octopus wolfi) in a Coral. Moalboal, Philippines (Shutterstock
1033935379); emperor dumbo octopus (*Grimpoteuthis imperator*)
© 2016 Alexander Ziegler

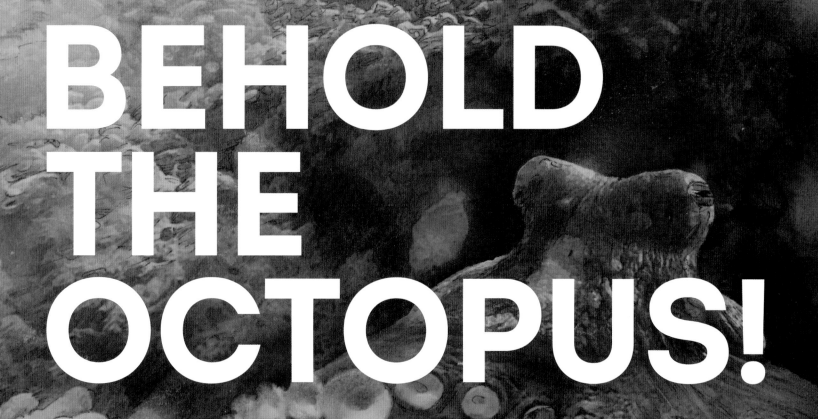

BEHOLD THE OCTOPUS!

Written by **SUZANNE SLADE**

Illustrated by **THOMAS GONZALEZ**

PEACHTREE

ATLANTA

Amazing octopus!

Eight long arms

swirl and curl

through salty seas . . .

An octopus doesn't have a single bone in its body. But it does have one small beak, two eyes, three hearts, and eight graceful arms. Octopuses are found in every ocean of the world. The common octopus (*Octopus vulgaris*) is the most studied species. Perhaps that's because these beautiful octopuses hang out in rather shallow waters on rocky coastlines where scientists can easily find them.

hunting,

Octopuses are clever hunters who often search for food at night. A hungry coconut octopus (*Amphioctopus marginatus*) patiently waits for tasty snacks to swim by—crab, shrimp, or fish. Then it pounces on its prey! The coconut octopus also hunts by foraging around rocks with its long arms. Sometimes it carries a seashell or a coconut shell for protection.

building,

Most octopuses live alone. This solitary animal enjoys hanging out in its den—a hole or crevice inside coral or rocks. The big blue octopus (*Octopus cyanea*) uses its powerful arms to build a den out of rocks. Sometimes it also fashions a rock door to keep other animals out and stay safe. The big blue octopus is a wanderer, moving into a new place about every month.

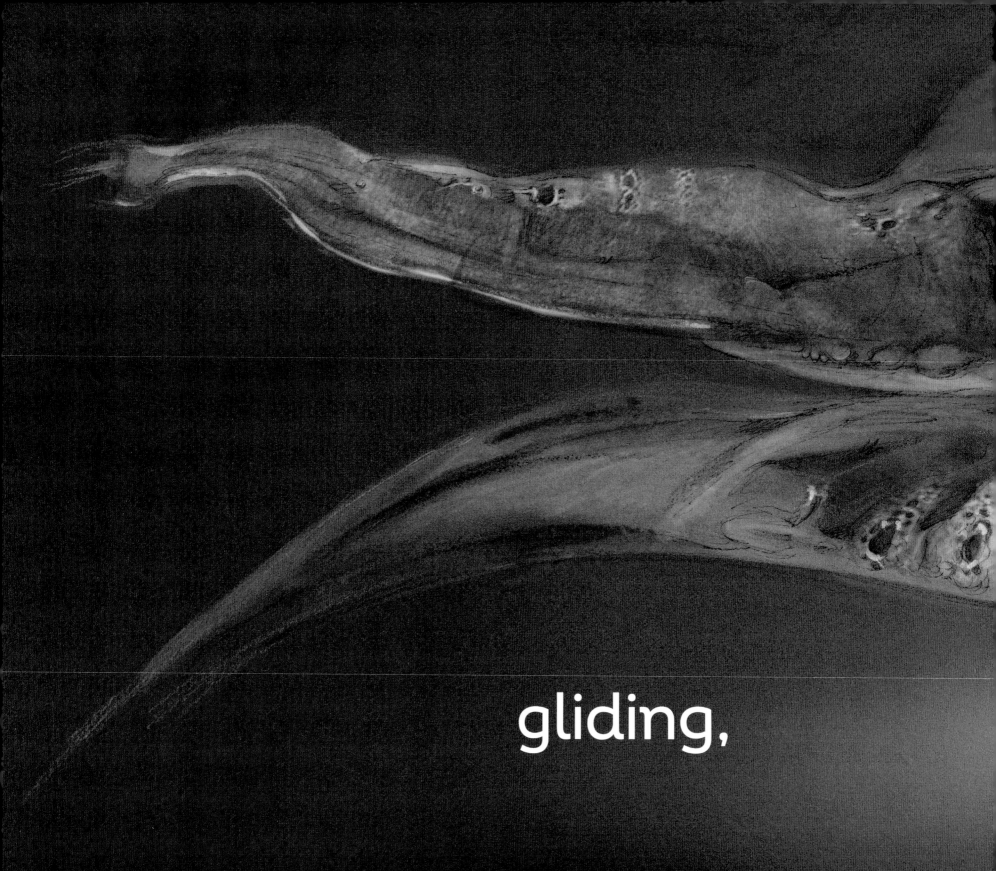

gliding,

An octopus uses water jets to push itself through the sea. It draws water into its body, then blasts it out through a tube called a siphon. The blanket octopus (*Tremoctopus violaceus*) spends a lot of time gliding across the open ocean. If a female blanket octopus meets predators on her journey, she may unfurl the gorgeous webbing between her arms to scare them off, or dive down to deeper waters for safety.

changing,

The octopus is an expert at fooling predators, changing its skin color and pattern to match its surroundings. This shape-shifter may even alter the texture of its skin to create the perfect camouflage. But the mimic octopus (*Thaumoctopus mimicus*) has another amazing trick. It can modify its appearance and behavior to impersonate another animal, such as a sea snake, lionfish, or flatfish.

grasping,

An octopus has dozens of strong suction cups on each arm, which it uses to move rocks or catch dinner. These suckers also provide a sense of touch and taste to help it find food. The largest octopus, the giant Pacific octopus (*Enteroctopus dofleini*), weighs an average of 100 pounds (45 kilograms). Its mighty suckers measure up to 2.5 inches (6.4 centimeters) in diameter and each one can hold 35 pounds (16 kilograms)!

hiding.

When in danger, an octopus releases black ink to hide and make a quick getaway from predators. The ink cloud can also irritate eyes and disrupt smell and taste, which usually stops enemies from attacking. As the Caribbean reef octopus (*Octopus briareus*) cruises the seas, it's always prepared to squirt an ink-black cloud of protection in case hungry fish and sharks appear.

Luminous,

The glowing sucker octopus (*Stauroteuthis syrtensis*) has small lights on the underside of each arm instead of sticky suckers. This rare, deep-sea creature uses these glowing lights to attract prey. Its reddish-brown skin is translucent, so its internal organs are visible.

dangerous,

Octopuses are carnivores—they eat meat such as clams, fish, and shrimp. After catching its prey, an octopus releases poisonous venom to stun or kill its dinner. The blue-ringed octopus (*Hapalochlaena lunulata*) may be small, but it's very powerful. Though its body is around the size of a golf ball, about 2 inches (5 centimeters) across, it produces extremely dangerous venom—potent enough to kill people. When hungry, the blue-ringed octopus wiggles an arm to imitate a worm and attract fish and crabs.

adventurous,

Octopuses are smooth and sleek, perfect for gliding through water. The algae octopus (*Abdopus aculeatus*) is also able to leave its watery home and walk on land. It uses the suckers on its arms to pull its slippery body over sand or rocks, as it moves from tide pool to tide pool searching for food.

and utterly tenacious!

After laying her eggs, a mother octopus guards them from predators. She stays by their side, day and night, waving her arms to move currents of fresh, oxygenated water over them. For many octopuses, this brooding time lasts months. But for the deep-sea octopus (*Graneledone pacifica,* or as previously known, *Graneledone boreopacifica*), brooding may continue for years because their eggs develop more slowly in the cold, deep-sea water. Soon after they hatch, the exhausted mother dies of starvation.

Behold,

the marvelous octopus

only lives a short time.

But until the very end,

a doting mother carefully tends

to her precious clutch of eggs.

And soon,

brave, new hatchlings

each set off all alone,

to make their own homes

in the sparkling seas.

A newly hatched octopus is quite
independent. It is able to swim, feed itself,
and even create ink. Though many hatchlings are eaten by
predators, those that survive later set up their own dens
where they happily live alone. An octopus usually lives from
six months to five years, depending on the species. Though an
octopus life is not very long, it's always full of adventure!
(young *Graneledone pacifica*)

THE AMAZING OCTOPUS

Octopuses are beautiful, adaptable, resilient, and very clever. This intelligent animal is able to use tools, remember locations, open jar lids, and even solve puzzles.

The octopus is also a master of disguise. Its skin contains chromatophores, tiny organs that allow the octopus to change its skin color and create patterns to blend in with its surroundings.

coconut octopus (*Amphioctopus marginatus*)

mimic octopus (*Thaumoctopus mimicus*)

An octopus doesn't have any bones, which means its flexible body can squeeze through small spaces, like the mouth of a bottle or a small hole on a boat.

But the octopus does have one hard structure: its beak, which it uses to puncture shells on clams, crabs, and other tasty crustaceans.

The octopus has another superpower. If it loses an arm, there's no need to worry. It can grow a new one! This regeneration process begins right away, and once grown, the new arm will be just like the original.

The amazing octopus varies greatly in size. The tiny star-sucker pygmy octopus (*Octopus wolfi*) is less than an inch long (2.5 centimeters) and doesn't even weigh as much as a paper clip, while the largest giant Pacific octopus (*Enteroctopus dofleini*) ever recorded was 30 feet (9.1 meters) across and weighed over 600 pounds (272 kilograms)!

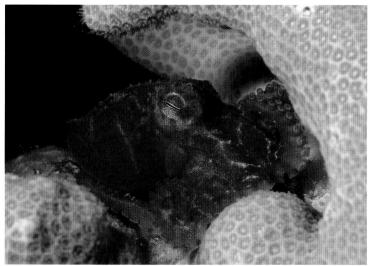
star-sucker pygmy octopus (*Octopus wolfi*)

There are about 300 different species of octopuses, but scientists are still discovering new ones, such as the emperor dumbo octopus (*Grimpoteuthis imperator*). Found in the North Pacific Ocean in 2016, this adorable creature has earlike fins and webbing between its arms.

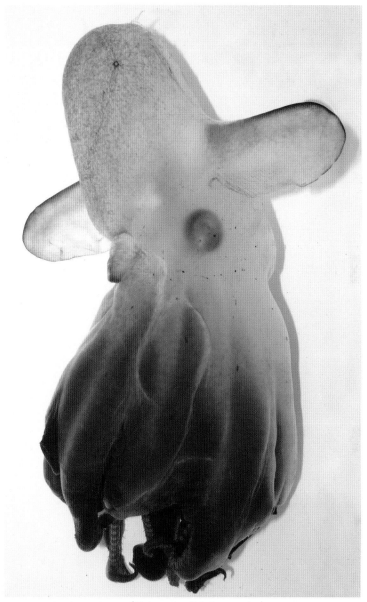
emperor dumbo octopus (*Grimpoteuthis imperator*)

Imagine the many fascinating octopuses yet to be discovered!

ACKNOWLEDGMENTS

Sincere thanks to Janet Voight, PhD, Associate Curator,
Life Sciences Division, Negaunee Integrative Research Center
at The Field Museum in Chicago, for reviewing and vetting
the content of this book.

LEARN MORE ABOUT THE OCTOPUS

"8 Marine Creatures that Light Up the Sea," *Discover Magazine*
www.discovermagazine.com/planet-earth/8-marine-creatures-that-light-up-the-sea

"Blanket Octopus," Great Barrier Reef Foundation
www.barrierreef.org/the-reef/animals/blanket-octopus

Duke, Cameron, "All hail 'Emperor Dumbo,' the newest species of deep-dwelling octopus," *LiveScience*
www.livescience.com/emperor-dumbo-octopus-deep-sea.html

"Mimic Octopuses," MarineBio Conservation Society
www.marinebio.org/species/mimic-octopuses/thaumoctopus-mimicus

"Deep-sea octopus broods eggs for over four years—longer than any known animal," Monterey Bay Aquarium Research Institute
www.mbari.org/deep-sea-octopus-broods-eggs-for-over-four-years-longer-than-any-known-animal

"Giant Pacific Octopus," *National Geographic*
www.nationalgeographic.com/animals/invertebrates/facts/giant-pacific-octopus

"Octopus," *National Geographic Kids*
kids.nationalgeographic.com/animals/invertebrates/facts/octopus

"Octopuses," National Wildlife Federation
www.nwf.org/Educational-Resources/Wildlife-Guide/Invertebrates/Octopuses

"A Coconut Octopus Uses Tools to Snatch a Crab," *Smithsonian Magazine*
www.smithsonianmag.com/videos/category/science/a-coconut-octopus-uses-tools-to-snatch-a-crab

"Ten Curious Facts About Octopuses," *Smithsonian Magazine*
www.smithsonianmag.com/science-nature/ten-curious-facts-about-octopuses-7625828

Animal Diversity Web, University of Michigan Museum of Zoology
animaldiversity.org

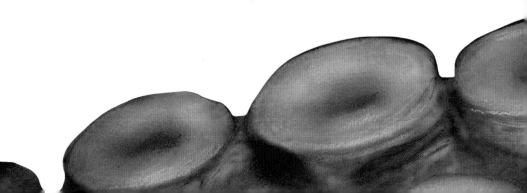

SELECTED BIBLIOGRAPHY

Courage, Katherine Harmon. "Common Octopus Proves Uncommonly Difficult to Define." *Scientific American*, August 29, 2014. *blogs.scientificamerican.com/octopus-chronicles/ common-octopus-proves-uncommonly-difficult-to-define.*

Courage, Katherine Harmon. "How Octopus Arms Regenerate With Ease." *Scientific American*, August 28, 2013. *blogs.scientificamerican.com/octopus-chronicles/ how-octopus-arms-regenerate-with-ease.*

Huffard, Christine L., Roy L. Caldwell, Ned DeLoach, David Wayne Gentry, Paul Humann, Bill MacDonald, Bruce Moore, Richard Ross, Takako Uno, and Stephen Wong. "Individually Unique Body Color Patterns in Octopus (*Wunderpus photogenicus*) Allow for Photoidentification." *PLOS ONE* (November 2008). *doi.org/10.1371/journal.pone.0003732.*

Richter, Jonas N., Binyamin Hochner, and Michael J. Kuba. "Pull or Push? Octopuses Solve a Puzzle Problem." *PLOS ONE* (March 2016). *doi.org/10.1371/ journal.pone.0152048.*

Robison, Bruce, Brad Seibel, and Jeffrey Drazen. "Deep-Sea Octopus (*Graneledone boreopacifica*) Conducts the Longest-Known Egg-Brooding Period of Any Animal." *PLOS ONE* (July 2014). *doi.org/10.1371/ journal.pone.0103437.*

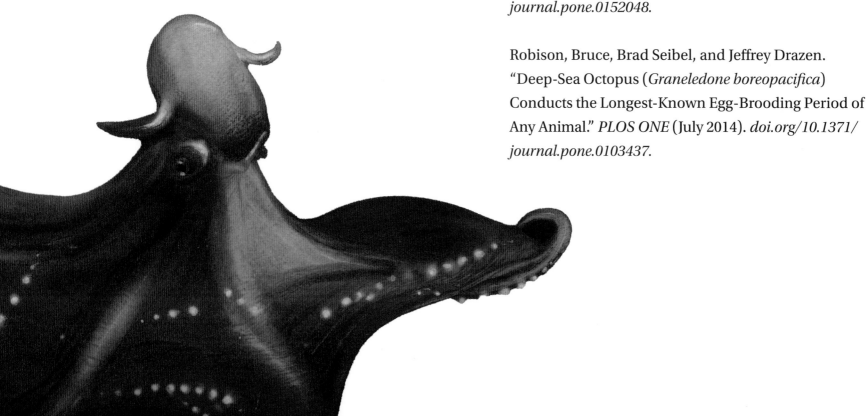

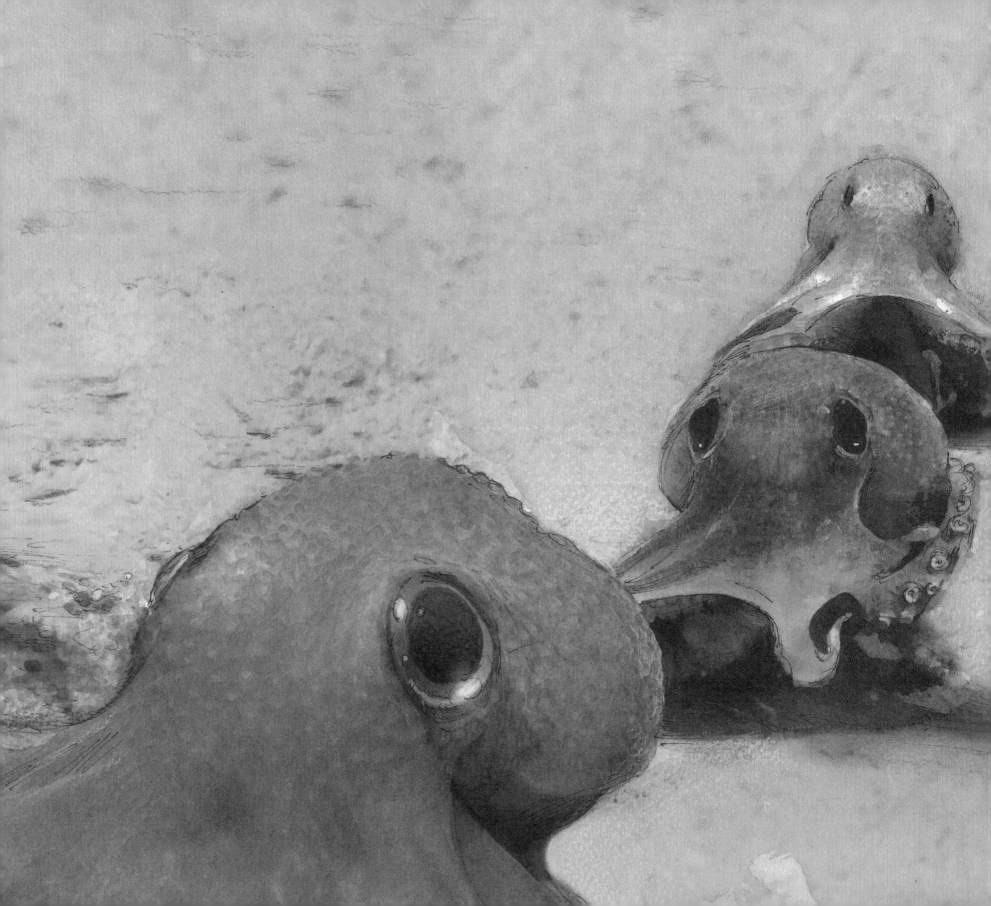